P9-EMC-122

ADVANCE PRAISE FOR *WE ARE MALALA*

In *We Are Malala,* accomplished poet Katerina Fretwell deftly compares and contrasts her path as a western young woman coming of age in the seventies to that of Malala Yousafzai, the young, Pakistani, Islamic advocate for the education of girls who won the Nobel Prize at the age of seventeen in 2012. Through the urgent flow of tightly interwoven Urdu-like couplets, west meets east, sister meets sister. Two histories of emerging feminism in different cultures intertwine. Fretwell's tribute to and celebration of Malala and her legacy expands to address the oppression of all people, commenting on the colonization of First Nations and abuses of the residential schools. Kat's and Malala's stories move readers from an "I" to a "we" perspective, enabling us to experience though the power of poetry the subtle and inextricable ways in which "United we thrive, divided we die./ All souls. All sentience.//"Sentenced to prescience, We Are Malala."
—SUSAN MCCASLIN, author of *Into the Open: Poems New and Selected*

Katerina Fretwell's *We Are Malala* is a celebration of shared identity as healing. Its breaths are ritual, personal, universal, and ecstatic. It lays itself down as a steady walk, with linked arms, into the darkness of the assassin's rifle barrel, giving it the light of bodily presence and continued life. It begs to be sung.
—HAROLD RHENISCH, author of *Two Minds*

Katerina Fretwell's *We Are Malala* entwines Malala Yousafzai's courageous life and struggles with the poet's own, then broadens to consider many historic and contemporary injustices, especially toward women. Malala, a young woman

who resisted and changed the world, becomes an emblem of what we all might strive for. An ambitious, powerful book.
—ELIZABETH GREENE, author of *Moving* and *A Season Among Psychics*

This tribute to an outstanding leader in the worldwide struggle for gender equality is deeply informed by the poet's own struggles. Katerina Fretwell weaves Malala's life story with hers in a tender dance of passionate youth and committed wisdom. A song of hope.
—SUSAN MCMASTER, author of *Until The Light Bends*

In her book, *We Are Malala*, Katerina Vaughan Fretwell champions the importance of the meeting of minds in a post-9/11 world troubled by the impulse to break into mutually exclusive hate-filled groups of us and them. To what might we aspire in this violent world? Fretwell reminds us how the poet of today might leave us a hint of the truth, not be found in mere information, but truth eternal, abiding, consoling, and hopeful, as she writes in the closing lines of her final poem, the heroic and eponymous "We Are Malala": "United we thrive, divided we die./All souls. All sentience./ Sentenced to prescience, We Are Malala."
—JOHN B. LEE, Poet Laureate of the city of Brantford in perpetuity, Poet Laureate of Norfolk County for life

WE ARE MALALA

poems and art by

Katerina Vaughan Fretwell

inanna poetry & fiction series

INANNA Publications and Education Inc.
Toronto, Canada

Copyright © 2019 Katerina Vaughan Fretwell

Except for the use of short passages for review purposes, no part of this book may be reproduced, in part or in whole, or transmitted in any form or by any means, electronically or mechanically, including photocopying, recording, or any information or storage retrieval system, without prior permission in writing from the publisher.

The publisher gratefully acknowledges the support of the Canada Council for the Arts and the Ontario Arts Council. The publisher is also grateful for the financial assistance received from the Government of Canada.

Front cover artwork: Katerina Vaughan Fretwell, "Malala," 2014, acrylic, 20 x 16 inches.

Library and Archives Canada Cataloguing in Publication

Title: We are Malala : poems and art / Katerina Vaughan Fretwell.
Names: Fretwell, Kathy, 1944- author, illustrator.
Series: Inanna poetry & fiction series.
Description: Series statement: Inanna poetry & fiction series
Identifiers: Canadiana (print) 20190094257 | Canadiana (ebook) 2019009429X | ISBN 9781771335850 (softcover) | ISBN 9781771335867 (epub) | ISBN 9781771335874 (Kindle) | ISBN 9781771335881 (pdf)
Subjects: LCSH: Yousafzai, Malala, 1997- — Poetry.
Classification: LCC PS8561.R47 W4 2019 | DDC C811/.54—dc23

Printed and bound in Canada

Inanna Publications and Education Inc.
210 Founders College, York University
4700 Keele Street, Toronto, Ontario M3J 1P3 Canada
Telephone: (416) 736—5356   Fax (416) 736—5765
Email: inanna.publications@inanna.ca Website: www.inanna.ca

To Malala, and to everyone, particularly girls,
struggling to get an education,
to my family who believed in the importance of education,
and to my legions of teachers and mentors.

Also by Katerina Vaughan Fretwell

Poetry:

Dancing on a Pin
Class Acts
Angelic Scintillations
Samsara: Canadian in Asia
Shaking Hands with the Night
Remyth
Apple, Worm and All
The Ultimate Contact

Edited poetry collections:

Arms Like Ladders
And no one knows the blood we share

Contents

Foreword

Shot because she envisioned schooling for girls. Eleven years old. What an extraordinary young girl, not even a teenager at the time! I revered middle-age Dr. Sima Simar for her bravery in standing up at gunpoint for female humanity, after reading Sally Armstrong's *Veiled Threat:Women of Afghanistan.* I also pored over Karen Armstrong's books about the three religions of Abraham. The events of 9/11 stoked my curiosity about all things Islamic. An eleven-year-old Pakistani girl risks her life for something I as a North American take for granted. I snapped up her book: *I Am Malala,* written by Malala Yousafzai with BBC journalist Christina Lamb. We are Malala, humanity as a whole, united—or else ... I quake at where we are heading.

Laden with acutely perceived details and a precocious grasp of politics, tribalism and motives, Malala's memoir consumed me. I hungered for intimate knowledge of Pashtunwali (Pashtun culture), Islam, and Mohammad, not to convert but to understand this fascinating foreign culture rich in poetic traditions and previous notable accomplishments. Malala's book fleshed out both Armstrong authors' forays into Islam from her Pashtun perspective; how people live, eat, dress, believe, play....

Her life, rich in ideas and astounding educational pursuits for age eleven, transcends the material hardships endemic to the Swat Valley region. A faithful Muslim, Malala professes that the misogynistic Sharia Law is outside the Qur'an and *hadith* (interpretations). Curiosity piqued, I read M.A.S. Abdel Haleem's translation of the Qur'an and basked in its poetry and kindnesses. Like the Torah (Old Testament) and Gospels (New Testament), the Qur'an demands fealty to the One God and abounds in historic struggles to assert itself. Likewise, heaven and hell come to life in vivid detail.

Culture-bound as one of the Peoples of the Book—Jews, Christians, Muslims, all descended from Abraham—I needed to learn about Muhammad, Prophet of Islam. Leslie Hazelton's *The First Muslim* and Martin Lings' *Muhammad* filled me in on this compassionate, long-suffering Holy Man.

Disclosure: I was raised Presbyterian, became Roman Catholic, and sang in Anglican/Episcopalian choirs. Now I am eclectic in internalizing whatever spirituality, Eastern, Western or ancient, helps me evolve.

As tensions stockpile in a steadily incendiary course after the 9/11 events, I think it is imperative for peoples of all beliefs to dialogue, understand, and accept one another. Not only are global hot spots proliferating, but our planet itself is in peril. For example, the Swat Valley, between the Hindu Kush section of the Himalayas, teemed with fruit trees and the River Swat, with trout. Wars, quakes, and floods have killed or displaced millions, decimated homes and schools into rubble, and polluted the river into rubbish. Unemployment and poverty breed hatred and desperate measures. Land, water, sky, and hearts can absorb only so much before becoming uninhabitable.

As a western feminist, I struggle with draconian laws that subdue, confine, and at times, torture and kill women. Malala forgave her shooter, a spiritual marvel for one so young, for anyone. In my poems, I leap into a foreign *dasein*: one's way of being-in-the-world. The power of imagination, factoring in my flaws and favouritism, is one best hope in overcoming our differences and celebrating our diversity. Unless otherwise noted, information from or about Malala that I interpret comes from *I Am Malala,* Malala's memoir, and quotes from the Qur'an.

In *We Are Malala,* I narrate my stories, and Malala's, mainly in couplets, as an envisioned bridge between our two solitudes, East and West. In so doing, I wish to foster our common humanity and capacity for intimate understanding and mutual respect.

Katerina Vaughan Fretwell, "Malala, from the photo by Insiya Syed,"
2019, acrylic, 14 x 11 inches.

Star Blessed and Crossed

So woe to ... those who are all show
and forbid kindnesses.
—Qur'an 107: 5-7

To me the meanest flower that blows can give
thoughts that often lie too deep for tears.
—William Wordsworth, *Intimations of Immortality*

I point to petals everywhere,
powdering, perfuming air.
Your town Gulkada: site of blooms.

Dear Malala, in awe, I'm drawn
like bee to nectar, your life

grace spirit — cereus abloom
once every century.

Star blessed, star crossed, named
Malala, for *Malalai of Maiwand,*

Afghan's Joan of Arc, your koan.
Malalai means *grief-stricken,*

thorny roses, Venus Fly-Trap, a mine
fielded by warring factions, let's bridge

our two solitudes. Breathe, dear one,
breathe even the dirt path to the Swat,

smell of dead fish, so far from
your homeland now, maybe never safe

for you. Pomegranates, peaches,
guavas, grapes, home sensed.

As dawn's final star faded, you arrived,
feted, despite being female in a family

reliant on oil lamps, outhouse, mud-walls.
Your lucky birth, July 12, 1997,

caring Cancer, bold Ox, propelled the ascension
to three rooms over your dad's school.

Running water, concrete walls. Kindnesses
papered your homestead like floral wallpaper.

As kids, we both reviewed daily news,
your fervent free-falling views,

unlike my era's youth — *seen, not heard,*
speak only when spoken to.

Your freedom walled in, mine
flowering inside my head.

*

Your play-ground, fecund Swat Valley
within Hindu Himalayan Kush,

I ponder as aching beauty,
an Eighth Wonder

out-sizing grey grassy
Rockies, snowy sundae Alps.

I proclaim

world heritage of all women,
your charmed childhood: so fleeting a hush

before you fell into crossfire, cross
purposes, almost crossed out.

Your village, once bursting floral,
your Eden, despite bleeding urchins'

stigmata-lesions from mounting
rubbish mounds, hoarding discards

to sell for room and food. You wish
for them free schooling,

I wished escape through education
for my former social-work clients.

But your dad cautioned: junkyard finds keep families fed.
How to help? You bet your life.

*

Malala, your parents' *Pashtunwali* hospitality

floods in your blood; swift as Swat in monsoon season.

I read how extremist Zia fossilized his rule in 1977 —
jailing the raped, not the rapists,

woman's word flipped over
girls' skipping stones,

woman's income vaulted into
male ramparts,

granite-chiseled texts re-sculpted
history,

region calcified into Fortress Islam —
not true Islam, not one pebble.

*

Our One-God prophets
didn't brick in religion,

they Spackle-d faith, compassion.
Why do we cement what ballasts

greedy egos, doubts mortared,
souls stone-cold right —

why not adamantly One, loving *all.*
Why not?

*

The gorge
between ideal real;

we are not worlds apart,
two Crabs who love late rising. Art

our conclusion, two Old Souls whose
birth numbers equal nine.

Two crustaceans swimming —
me, upstream, you in riptides.

*

Two stuttering dads; yours birthed schools,
mine enshrined

in the library bearing his name: Harold Campbell Vaughan,
Acadia University, Wolfville, Nova Scotia.

Portals to learning bind us
in dawn's fluorescence.

Malala, like your birth,
mine also feted —

miracle — haunted by five stillbirths, Mom
at seven months bed-perched, confined to chamber pot.

Me, three weeks preemie. *Road not taken,*
war-baby, Mom's hysterectomy:

twenty stores ransacked for formula:
no breast milk post-surgery.

Can't believe I was skinny till age nine —
we love our food.

*

We're steeped in free-range chicken dung.
I moved farm to town; you, above school.

You played rooftop cricket. I climbed down
treed sun-porch, banished for backtalk.

Signed Independence Declaration
in blood, still forced into prep-school.

Backtalk, yes. Elite girls' schools raised my hackles.
Scarce girls' schools reared your action.

Justice our table talk.

Preppies on silver platter, Tiffany-bound,
Pashtun girls on table, *burka*-bound.

*

The Qur'an decrees:
Those who have been attacked
are permitted to take up arms because

6

they have been wronged.
Musharraf, Mullah waylay this verse.

Think Russian *samizdat.* You've camouflaged
your schooling, yet fulfilled

your impulse

and defiance — henna-ing
your hands in calculus syllabus.

At eleven, you raised the spectre
of blitzed schools

on national radio with a no-show
militant hiding in a no-name

prerecorded spiel, too cowardly
to face a wee, unarmed *girl.*

Your dad lifted a baby girl
before a cowed crowd:

implored them to give girls
teacher and textbook lifelines.

Like raptors, locals looted local schools.

*

In Ramadan, *"believers"* preyed
on the unprotected

despite Qur'an veto on first strike,
bashed schools, trashed power-lines,

leaving people bereft: no gas, heat,
no water, no cholera quarantines,

kith, kin, country cannibalized.
You, pals jolted like ex-cultists,

bounties on your heads, duct-tape on your lips.
Falsely pious cannibalize Islam:

bait switch, master tactics.
Your town, school, valley static dump.

*

Our tentacled, timeless
gender disparity

bottom feeds despite three
waves of feminism.

I mourn all womanhood removed
from public life. Self-appointed

Mufti desiring girls in *purdah,*

erased under *burkas,*

tried to shutter your dad's school.
He called Mufti's bluff,

told him not to read scandal
in boys' and girls' playtime.

A private joke — your dad's student,
Mufti's niece.

*

Yet witness campus crimes:
despite affluence, abuse occurs.

Herd-think, compliance-drugs. Jocks rant: *Rape, rape!*
at campus sports as if *freshettes*,

for first time away
from home, are rendered pork-fat,

as if thrown under a *burqa* —

invisible, saran-wrapped at the supermarket,
like a biblical woman stoned at the well.

Frats who poll pledges in secret ballots:
Who do you fantasize raping? Drugging the punch,

stripping victim's will,
cloaking intent, violence   with silence.

University heads veil bad PR,
sweep victims under bottom line.

Your sisters' cloth *burkas*

are mindsets in the West, Malala,

thought-propelled burkesque.

Police pin mini-skirted sling-backed plaintiffs
on rap sheets:

You asked for it. All women
know *Slut Walk en camera*

defuses f-word: feminism.

                                        *

Travesty, third world girls beg for books;
western girls beg to be taken seriously.

Boys girls' piercings tats shout:
Notice me; I exist.

                                        *

Let's rule airtime, Sister. At prep-school,
Pam and I jived to *The Prophet:* a twist,

shocking Western All or Nothing
mindset: just one

allowed to be Number One,
the rest, wallflowers in Miss Darling's

ballroom, dancing — one couple
demo-ed for class. We gathered dust:

no room to be — no room
to be human, becoming us, Malala.

Gibran dancing Joy-Sorrow, Moon-Sun,
Man-Woman: *pas de deux* not Cartesian

but twirled tangoing talk into tiers:
gossip   events   ideas — whirled. Girls.

I hear whirled.
I hear world.
I hear whorled.

*

I hear cancer. It vaulted drunken kin
six feet down. Sorrow my Familiar,

Joy foreign. Gloom my homing pigeon.
Fate tries to dictate women drop a stitch,

do se do. Whorled. Sashaying *beaux*
into country barnyard dance

finally *je se jeter* Light vs Dark.

Sorrow *AND* Joy-Sorrow
my completion *the good, the bad,* Malala,

given do-or-die choice:
we channel our Inner Stalin.

*

Now Russian Bear claws at Ukraine.
Putin sticks pins into maps: caviar voodoo.

I recall my American History —
World War I divvying spoils

but FDR's New Deal helped, day by day,
folks stayed alive, day by day's fated coil.

Yet praising FDR's rescue —
earned me a C. *Stopgap only,*

declared my conservative teacher —
history schooled against

Democracy: rule *for* the people,
of the people, *by* the people.

Malala, you embody democracy,
light-bearer to girls on society's bottom rung.

*

Out of curtained memories
rise prep-school dance mixers,

giggles at wriggling drapes.
Couplings

hidden from chaperone;
wayward dates behind folds,

taunting: *Do **It** With Thy Might*
our school motto,

not FDR's discredited safety-net,
Churchill's *Iron Curtain:*

Fight Red's pinko socialism,
martyring maligned Rosenbergs —

not Russian spies but shot anyway,
casting a pall.

The War to End All Wars (WWII)
fertilized by Crash Depression

Dust-Dirty Thirties blowing
families onto streets,

refugees clinging to Liberty's beacon,
friend's parents escaping Hitler's *Beer Hall Putsch* —

for New Deal.
I know your fatwa, Malala: live

each day as the last which was first.
Whistle-blowers in the wind.

Life Magazine bellowing *Study hard as Russians study.*
I crammed four hours' slog

to Khrushchev pounding
his shoe on the UN podium: *Better Red than Dead.*

Your grandchildren will be communists.
It's curtains, Malala, *Bang, Bang,*

I cannot forget
all that hammering.

*

My childhood games
your rooftop cricket

mirror adult fear:
lead or be led, kill be killed,

Kahlil Gibran's middle way
marries opposites'

symbiotic fox-trot.

*

Buddhist Eightfold Path,
Golden Mean, Taoist detachment

spotlight our instincts,
jinxed whirling dervishes.

Didn't pre-Pakistan harbour Hindus
playing up Oneness?

In *Simon Says,*
to advance, whether dance, giant,

baby step, don't forget to ask:
Mother,

may I? Or forfeit.

Hindus, Muslims ... dance today
haram, sinful, wallflowers all —

Our mothers, may we

To Allah, in a Bottle

The only purpose for which power can be rightfully exercised over any member of a civilized community, against his will, is to prevent harm to others.
        —John Stuart Mill, *On Liberty*

Taught from infancy that beauty is woman's sceptre, the mind shapes itself to the body.
        —Mary Wollstonecraft, *A Vindication of the Rights of Woman*

Musharraf hallowed concerts, hollowed

the Law that raped

women must procure male
kin witnesses.

Malala, I was there, I swear.
All women were there.

It's still the victim on trial.
Sharing pain shame

with sister victims
on Facebook

is called collusion,
acquitting

the talk show host preferring
non-consensual rough-sex.

*

That's not the half of it:
bin Laden's ghost hovers.

Taken out by U.S. Navy Seals,
his hideout revealed Musharraf,

post 9/11, hid bin Laden
in Swat Valley, diverted

U.S. aid for his palace, yet hired
women to broaden the news.

*

Do you see bin Laden's shade,
Malala? Your dad abhorred

ghost schools lining pockets: ghost

principals, ghost teachers.
Ghastly. Padded. Who

do *you* trust, Malala,
haunting all discussions.

*

Musharraf's palace gilded,
bejewelled among hovels.

Unhooked bin Laden's Number Two,
but strung along Western reporters,

unclasped Pakistan to jihadists
of all facets, ignored junkyard squatters.

We're all strung out but most folks'
flaws string up only a few. Not dictators.

*

You set adrift a prayer
to Allah, in a bottle,

homing into refuse refuge
that was sacred Swat River.

Still your current of faith sweeps girls

up from shanty towns
stagnant, quicksand Destiny.

Remember 1947. Pakistan's
founder
Jinnah shaped a fissure to rive Mosque and

State in first Muslim country: no prayers
in ruling, no ruling on prayers.

*

> *You who believe, do not wrongfully consume*
> *each others wealth but trade by mutual consent....*
> *Do not covet what God has given to some of you*
> *more than others — men have the portion they*
> *have earned and women have the portion they*
> *have earned.*
> —Qur'an, 4:29 and 4:32.

Oh, Malala, that '05 quake —
extremists spliced Musharraf's half-knot

rescue into a ring-buoy
tossed to folks thrilled

to be famous on Mullah FM, unaware
the Head broadcast their sins

for reprisal, damned druggies
funding his guns.

*

And like the book-burning, medieval monk,
Head Mullah torched the culture banning

beauticians barbers Bollywood.
Public flogging: the new spectacle.

The Garden gutted
under a convenient quake. Don't underestimate perfidy.

Your town, *Mingora,* reduced
to an eyesore. Foetid flesh. Fallen citrus.
How alien, calamity.

Your textbooks: math, physics,
English, Urdu, Pashto, chemistry,

biology, *Islamiyat,* Pakistani
left behind.

Internally displaced,
at fourteen you're adult,

no giggling behind-drapes
prom queen.

No safe house to prolong childhood.
Maybe you're lucky

soldiers can't read write;
books — their outhouse wipes.

*

Malala, a hit-man rules Pakistan.
School dropout. Look at you.

Healing from head-shots, exiled in Birmingham,
loved ones, mother-tongue, neon-buses,

favourite buttered-chicken — a hemisphere
away. How on earth do you persevere.

*

Ironic, Islamabad's Red Mosque
students scorched brothels boutiques —

the army torched these girls
their Mosque to kingdom come.

Who's to say which tribe
carries inbred immunity. I don't.

*

Let me remember for you — for us.
On your birthday, Swat's Mullah

trounced Musharraf, denounced
arts *haram:* sinful, un-Islamic.

On your birthday, he blasted
ancient Buddhist shrines,

Bollywood your beloved. *Haram.*
All delights *haram.* Laughter *haram.*

*

Fear travels even here.
Consider Rashim's fate.

In Kingston, Ontario, I ate
in his *Pakistani Diner*

glued to Bollywood
cinema romancing the class climb,

Himalayan backdrop. Arts
threaten surreal: artists *feel*.

Afraid of inmates, Rashim resigned
from prison, set up his diner,

bragged of back-home *ghazal* poetry
all-nighters, ex-pat clinging to films,

killed if he returns.

Like you, exiled, homesick.
Bollywood is Kingston.

Ghazals capture mood, but often
brood over, rather than soften, our trials.

                                    *

What they learn, what they never learn.
Heads bobbing to the cadence,

madrasa sons inhale the Qur'an,

learning science literature trick them

into sin — U.S. plot. Memorize but don't
understand the Qur'an —safely, in Arabic

not Pashto, not in motherly
tongue, no link to enlightenment,

no bridge to real piety. It's not what they learn.
Heads bobbing to the cadence of what they never learn.

*

Here, too, Malala. People who swear each word's
gospel, suffer through conflicting stories.

How much of Jesus' message is his?
How much of Malala's is yours?

Sally Armstrong's book on distorted Islam
chaining daughters to brooms

drudgery, no sunlight enlivening bones blood.

I revere Benazir, don't you?
Sole leader to condemn Osama.

Bhutto governed longer gladly
than Britain's Iron Lady madly.

White dove perched on her shoulder, but,
still Benazir lost her life.

You stand like her, also shot.
White feathers float...

*

It is written: *Husbands should take good care of their wives.*

What of wives unable to read signs —
they'd be killed in traffic

like people everywhere thumbing smart-phones
in front of buses.

Your aunt couldn't picnic on Karachi beach.
A mourning dove wheels in the wind.

*

Pakistan's founder Jinnah wept at Muslim
refugees harassing Pashtuns.

Sunni versus Shia. Your brothers
steeped in blood, intimately

suffocating in blood; civil war's
uncivil mayhem.

If Viscount Mountbatten knew Jinnah
was dying, he'd leave India

drawn quartered, no sign
of a dove, no Muslim Pakistan.

No state hived off India
for Hindi peace.

Maps: rulers' colouring books.
Apartheid the faithful.

*

I have no experience of living
under the sharp-shooter's shadow,

but you know written spoken words
get you killed. A journalist calls

Pakistan the deadliest country ...
(for) a journalist.

*

And for women: Schooling allowed only
for girls not yet blooming. You pretended to be ten,

wore no school-clothes, stuck books in shawls,
hennaed-hands hidden in folds.

Your dad demanded cameras be hidden,
fearing your exposure to gunslingers

who claimed schooling westernizes.
You retorted: *Humanizes.*

According to Ban Ki-Moon Pakistan's
dire flood equalled a *slow-motion tsunami.*

What a sink hole:
how do we rise above water-torture,

how do we watermark reality,
no longer victims submerged

by terrorists too fear-logged to question,
by journalists too embedded to rise?

*

Kurt Eichenwald verified lies and
secrets post-9/11 in his book *500 Days.*

Dubya and cronies dammed the U.S.
Constitution, Geneva Conventions —

drowning detainees to the point of death
to force *'fessing up* —

but their frontier hubris backfired,
detainees faked facts to arrest

water-boarding torture
condoned in civilized society.

Katerina Vaughan Fretwell, "Malala, from photo by Antonio Olmos," 2014, watercolour, 11 x 8 inches.

Short Shrift and Swat Shot Sestina

Sister, do you recall
solo, sandy footprints,

a power lifting us?
Short shrift, wasn't it?

Despite lofty parents
we both stopped growing

at thirteen. *Sacre bleu,* I grew
aware of right wrong —

wide-angles of my town derailed,
train-tracks truncating

Catholic, Protestant playgrounds.
Hosti de tabernac, ratings: my god's

pur laine. Thanks be to Allah that's
not your story. Mom plopped me

into prep-school, cleaved from Catholic
best friend. But your footprints,

God's, uplift the citrus girl
marking sales with an X:

throwaway Lite Brite. Who needs
to read write.

Rebels soldiers: all devils. You mourned —
thug shot a man for not showing

his ankles below his trousers, then shot
man's father for being his *aba*, father.

How do you get inside a thug's thick head?

                                 *

Cops police cops, spring their own.
Remember *Trayvon,* unarmed, black.

Military brass, Head
Holies always spared ... never

at gunpoint, never held to reason,
never jailed ... never aware.

Casting your life to the winds —
snaring danger with each shared

thought, tall orders: your Girls
Foundation rattles your parents,

convinced Pashtuns revere the dead,
not the living, praying

each time you walk out the door,

29

speak on talk radio.

Flickering shadows threaten —
now you're heard world-wide.

*

Here's my Shot Swat Sestina,
here's me listening, Malala:

> Twenty-twelve, October nine
> defiant change —
> Malala, on the bus
> met hatred head-on
> while extolling school:
> who'd top the class?
>
> Best pupil in class,
> whizzed through all nine.
> Hungry for girls in school
> unlike shooter's deranged
> lust: *Girls, homestead-on,*
> *burka-defined, no more bus —*
>
> *only boys rate books, bus.*
> He singled you from class,
> shot you head-on.
> Your life on the line
> for all girls — arranged
> on global news — hope rules.
>
> You shared your study tools

with pals on the bus —
aching to short-change
burka-views *outside* class.
To the UN, you redefined
half of humanity head-on.

Cooling tribal thirst for heads on
poles, teachers' blood pooled —
school for those inclined
fearsomely foreign. On the bus
in cross-hairs, sighted-lass,
you sought whole shooting-range —

surefire, volcanic change
for *Pashtunwali* dead-on —
all females seasoned with class
nevermore unschooled.
Your dad no fear fuss
prompted girls, you in grade Nine

already a seismic change: schooled
this long heads-on in bus —
in class till *month ten, day nine.*

Day nine, life on the line
different endings.

Better than widow
maker —
better than window dresser.

So much at stake —

you, your dear ones

nailed to our consciousness,
our conscience.

*

In that family photo,
standing behind your new home

in Birmingham, I see you clone
your mom's painterly grin, high-born

flared nose, mellow cheeks chin
sepia-ringed irises — yet less

stoic, more questing,
firmer featured,

stepping out, your face on display,
your counter-point

to thugs blaming CIA
for schooling girls

and your father's sin:
not fencing you in.

*

If my poems landed in insurgents' hands,
would I copy you or clutch

a pseudonym — death
threatened daily till you didn't

know your name, country, life.
We fight to keep meaning alive.

Washed up on shore —
three-year-old Alan Kurdi almost

touched the promised land.

*

It takes one photo, one dead toddler
to galvanize the globe.

I'd have to be under fire to see
if I'd retract or fire back.

Nellie McClung and Famous five
weathered verbal hailstorms,

stood for a tectonic shift: The Law
admitting Women legally exist.

Mom graduated Columbia Law, 1932,
one of three women, estate lawyer.

After her death, her sister's sherry-
immersion, I ran to Granddad's,

changed nations during 'Nam,
now a provincial move shakes me.

Your skin knows Jeanne d'Arc's agony
flames rose, no recant.

What Marian calm, *Teresa of Avila,*
Sor Juana Inez de la Cruz

sidestepped their Inquisitors.

*

In 1968, I apprehended five children, warded off
the mother's fists — restrained by a john —

aftershocks, I dove into a wine-skin,
collapsed on my couch.

You story world-wide,
light up the unlettered,

pull down pompous pharisees.
Short shrift? Small in stature? Lift.

Walk tall,
Beacon in Lectern Lights.

Hope's Handmaiden. Saint Elizabeth
dispensing bread revealing roses.

Arma(geddon) Get Going

Malala, Michael Crichton thought
cyberspace meant *the end of our species,*

end of breath, you, me,
critters fending off death, tending to life.

The Western morbid craving for apocalypse —
arachnophobia lock-view on tarantula.

Long ago Hopi foretold we would flare
out *when a web covers the world,* and...

*

...here we are. Webbed.
Not Ariadne's tapestry or spider's art

but sound-waves crisscross our parted world,
wiring species to die every second. Shaky

sex-traders find johns online,
on corners worldwide, no AIDS checkpoints.

Sub-humanized drones
paint radium, go down with the burn.

MindCraft squares trees, pigs, bots onscreen,
between-lines grass-green sky-blue geometry.

Styrofoam-cellophane mothers
chops, cutlets. Bandwidth

madness, two techies
texting each other, sitting on same sofa

*

One mama, without mat leave, working her womb
herself to the still-point — stillborn.

Pregnant Maid, flogging three McJobs
to feed her family in America,

affording *Doritos* for lunch, flopped,
womb tipping, blood dripping, miscarrying.
No medical, no benefits. Barbara

Ehrenreich's *Nickel and Dimed* flags this. This:
fine *Nike's* earning a worker pennies

selling on upscale *Rodeo Drive*
hundred bucks a stitch.

I recycle clothes at Value Village,
no wardrobe malfunctions.

*

Or will we marvel at cobwebs,
our spirits evolved buffed beyond

binary bytes tweeted talk,
aware of global glare

care limned in love?
The UN didn't care

about safe toilets. *The Walrus*
magazine rolls:

191 countries [sloughed off sanitation
as a] Millennium Development Goal.

You could tell them a thing or two.
No private loos, long queues.

Sanitation's serious business.
A fourth of the world can't take

a clean crap — fertilizing field forest
with fecal fungi. Like Pakistani plumbing,

constipated towns outhouses
lands wells

still left to feed us.

*

Up shit creek without a paddle —
easy joke, hard probe.

Diarrhoea culling a million children
yearly. Imagine: a thousand

a thousand times. Please add
Hygiene to girls' curriculum, Malala.

What an addition.
We've covered this topic.

*

Till our next rout of the runs,
crappiest route the Rapture.

Your Prophet Muhammad prophesied Apocalypse.
He also spoke of ... the signs:

excessive height of buildings,
children's disrespect for parents.

Schoolboys priming family screen-time
with Ka-Pow blood-guts superheroes.

Seniors scammed of credit credibility
condos stacked sky-high over the homeless.

We make Revelation a game
dismissing devastation, voting in

white supremacists bricking walls
over asylum seekers, melting ice-caps,

embodying end-times.
Action our distraction,

while hackers a hemisphere away
shift our mice, wobble our Windows.

*

It ought to be *haram:* sinful.
Link-ups kink-ups winking

equally on Facebook & Twitter:
signing an activist petition

drooling in porn-filled perdition
Date Rape Drugs plastering women onscreen.

Our sisters *Bell Jarring*
into the drink, unthinkingly

deleting themselves —
no recycle bin,

no data retrieval, lost

ghosted in cyberspace.

Back in the trenches — Hindu Kush
switchbacks, heart-wrenching.

*

On Highway 400 in my *Honda Fit* —
out of nowhere a heart-stopping THUNK...

THUD. Cars racing off, paranoia flooding
me: is my blasted *Good Year* contagious.

Kind couple, alert clerk tossing
a lifeline. Wiling my wait with *Canadian Living*.

Tired tire-man surmising pranksters
placed spikes on highway for a lark.

What *Schadenfreude* malarkey
exudes pleasure in carnage's spark.

                                        *

Some females are too public,
damned, deleted. Our media is not

social but in wild impunity asocial,
embracing evil opportunity

when behaviour's off-radar, boxed
in steel or screen: immune. In WIFI's

remote-controlled-worlds even
friendship can't unfurl, let alone

bone-curdling pitch, shill,
scam, grift, sales bustle hustle.

Have you heard the joke:
selling snow to Eskimos,
Malala?

Like Afghans
selling sand.

I bonded, beyond the pitch
for my third leased Honda Fit.

Now seller's gaunt grey. His story,
my story, individual ends: Cancer.

Peter says his wife's on her second battle.
I say cancer seconded Jack's death-rattle.

No longer seller and buyer, we stared
at Armageddon rising inside us,

I'm terrified of Michael Crichton
who died of throat cancer —

a prophet, he inhaled our hatred
for reminding us we're finite.

Absorbed-anger ate him from within.
West's denial of death a tumour

of the soul, capricious culture
kicking aging stars off-stage,

enriching cosmetic doctors,
hiding the hopeless in hospice,

refusing assisted death to those
who've long ago lost joy —

sitting in shit swallowing
gall, dignity invaded by Trolls.

My culture's sick, Malala.
At least yours honours old people,

not caching them in hospital
turning elder-care over to paid staff.

*

Poorly-paid, no stock in caring jobs.
Mate's end-times tilted my world.

Vultures circling, poised.
Visibly ill, Jack craved a cool car.

Dealer drooled. Dodge glinted, gold.
I couldn't deny him rapture

over the vehicle's heated seats.
Unable to eat, even sing

over soap bubbles, his life whittled
down to changing pillows

to ease his pain while glossing *The Toronto Star.*
Six months later, he died,

passing on twenty-grand loan I hadn't co-signed.
Fate's aftershocks

of Jack's estate socked me. The bank,
choked me: *Pay.*

Bereft, I quaked at threats
my pricey lawyer said, *Ignore.*

Finally the bank cranked back.

*

Jack's miniscule
thrill in his end-stage is rage.

The West projects golden appliances
for every citizen steak.

It buries hurt, which is less:
template for woes   loneliness.

*

Westerners still spool faith
in above-board connections.

Aching to believe, living by our leave,
wincing at trauma

flogged to boost ebbing print media.
Craving feel-good stories bios

where badness flames out.
The media creates madness,

ogling mammoth print-runs sales,
poetic diction full of fictions

sounding nothing at all:
No fury, no existential roar.

Every summit, every bestseller cracking
open raw hope —

losing love to metastasis, looking to you,
Malala. Your global view,

fluid not static: your higher
self hefting the bereft

kick-boxing ego aside,
outward-eye seeking to salve —

not in halves, not as heroine,
just as a woman muttering

against false Rapture,
praying raptors' greed ruptures.

*

Forget stalkers. You carry light —
Birmingham mother, her daughter

raped at a Rave, sending
twenty pounds for hope you raise.

Mumbai girl gifting
rupees for teachers textbooks,

after the sale of bangles
her dad bought her, sharing

what her learning illumined.
Girl in Peshawar selling

her *shalwar* to spread your loving fund.
Tunisian set himself on fire.

His funeral pyre
blazed Death to Demagogues. Spark

igniting regime after regime.
Hordes huddled in Tahrir Square

tweeted like phoenixes finding song.
Social media's democrats: outcasts cast out iconoclasts.

*

My home's rural as your Swat Valley,
yet one click on my laptop connects

me to creators anywhere. You too,
working with girls written-off

in remote, refugee enclaves.
To you, to this, this easiness,

my gratitude is infinite. Our song:
Armageddon, bygones, begone.

How It Starts

I wager you'd allow bombs' anti-lullaby
blasting you to sleep — to be home.

Army versus Rebels   supernovas your valley —
moonscape, distorting Mosque State.

Each side eclipses other —
calls itself Allah's Chosen.

*

No one foretold Hitler's Final Solution.
Brother sub-humanized into *Other,*

convicted yet puzzled by victim-hood,
seething like silencer on handgun's muzzle:

shoving a hood over *Its* face,
missing *its cri de coeur,* powder trace.

*

Take Sarajevo before the Bosnian War —
Jews Christians Muslims broke bread

communally. Enter fear —
mountainside gardens of skulls.

*

I've been Presbyterian, Roman Catholic,
Anglican chorister. Beliefs intrigue me —

stories about time place — hubris Narcissus,
obstacle Minotaur, historian Ariadne.

*

Tree leaf cloud conversant to receptive ancients,
kinder to women, Malala,

than both our beliefs
bottle-fed us as youngsters.

One-God systems cut the cord,
women pagans stillborn, flesh bedevilled.

Luther, by surprise, grew a new religion
battling the devil in St. Elizabeth's gatehouse.

Wesley, Knox regimented women
as monstrous, Mary of Magdela was fired

as First Apostle, demoted to harlot.
Brave padres ordain females,

sponsor LGBTQ cafés, marry gays.
It's a start. Goddess Astarte has her ways.

*

Church boarding schools savaged First Nations

glued their tongues for speaking heritage,
called it Saving Souls.

Winnipeg's Mayor Bowman gave the Cree
a voice in governance, but Aboriginals

still fill jails — today's residential schools.
It's not inmates who are fools. I tally:

*

Testing Testing Debutante Tea 1962
subtitled How To Snag Lord Stag.

Chez A Priori Interrogator's, I quail,
her Brahmin, Dowager voice minked frail:

> Token-preppie non-wasp beau — fail.
> Fatherless in drunken milieu — fail.
>
> Two widowed sisters, two brats — fail.
> No social links, manners flat — fail.
>
> Paternal famous surgeon — pass.
> No Lord, Lady lineage — fail.
>
> Ethnic friends, ballroom skills — half fail.
> Attends Wells not Wellesley — half pass.
>
> Mother missed Our Formal Tea — fail...
> *But my mother is dead* — I wail.

49

Maternal family bankrupt — fail.
Paternal grand donation — overpass.

Today, Ladies, Lords, Debs, I pass
on to you: if our society fails,

since we're all conjoined, we will fail
to have high tea to pass on…

*

Mom picked her '30's brown frock for my debut.
Aunt Kate stated: *"No. At least give her proper armour."*

Mom begged proper white for me: *Cinderella.*
No glass slipper, a glass ceiling clipped my wings.

No arts. *Too flaky,* Mom said, glaring into her sherry. In May,
months before Debut Testing Testing Tea,

Mom died, willing me to her sister —
to Granddad's furor my aunt's terror.

I slung Christmas bulbs on a bush
to silence my soused aunt. She snored

on kitchen floor, stained robe mounding
Gallo belly. Yet I loved her.

How could I kowtow to a group
whose worth was a birth accident?

Who looked through me, not giving two hoots
grief swallowed me whole.

I ran to Canada.
I chose my country.

*

At last I had my say, Malala.
Your Qur'an states:

*anyone, male or female, who does good
deeds and is a believer, will enter Paradise...*

Those who are forced to let others think,
believe their compliance

proves they are alive, alert
to each pert facial intone

as the oppressed often are,
psyching out their rulers' moods

to live another day.

Saddam feigning no-fear,
deploying his subjects' terror as his own.

*

Our experts build human blood, organs, skin,
but our souls are light-years in arrears.

How do we stop spooking Sandy Hook,
Darfur, Mingora, Aleppo.

The Robespierre Reign of Terror revealed:
revolutions eat their own,

Malala.   Let   Us   Not
Become   What   We   Fear.

*

Last century the West wagered
The War To End All Wars.

Your land trampled, Malala,
desecrated ruptured flooded.

My land untrammelled for two
long centuries now drownings in the Gulf.

*

In your lifetime, Greenland's glaciers
will be salt water: seas up seven metres,

cosmopolitan coasts, first canaries:
unsuspecting Inuit wolves huskies

howling at oily toxic auroras.
Third World nations scapegoated

for western fervour, sacred-cows' methane.

Beef-cattle graze on former rainforests
while k.d. lang from cow country

sings against the sirloin-fad.
What happened to Sixties' protests?

*

Folksong hootenannies, silliest safest ditties:
Minnie lost her morals down among the corals
but oh she was good to me, well-a, well-a, well-a...

till fisher-folks' seines snared coral reefs.
Calls for amends flood us. I'm sorry.

*

I know too well how it starts —
residual guilt fear from theft

of Indigenous land humanity, Malala.
With the will, we'll bring them back, and us.

Wham, Bam, *Haram*

Why deny: *...the cry*
of Allahu Akbar

is a reminder to balance
our agency with humility

wrote Irshad Manji.

What is being denied here.
Who is crying?

I visualize frightened females
crushed under extremists' Sharia

Law — distorted or truly anti-female —
what percentage of the world's women live

in the valley of the shadow of death?

                          *

That translates as a shopping list for a wife
common as a bombed mosque:

> "I want wide pelvis pecs,
> no backtalk, eyes downcast.
>
> Can't read, peruse news.
> Comes with gold bangles — sold

according to my whim. No kohl
lip-gel, no shaved legs pits.

At daybreak, she curries bakes.
In famine, my sons and I partake

but she and her girls forsake food.
If they don't make it, well — *Inshallah*
(God willing).

If only men afraid of women knew
of *Khadija,* old widow,

entrepreneur, primary love
of The Prophet's entire life.

*

Serfdom's thriving here in Canada
according to *Macleans Magazine.*

First: *… military … punishes the women
who denounce their rapists.* And:

*Sixteen years ago … the military promised
changes.* We wait.

Not patiently. Patiently,
the army lobs bromides,

cages outrage in civil,
not military, court. Sensitivity

training: kill first, question
later. Obedience

ground into broken-ankle
double-time marching,

each crop of Honeys notched
to stay alive on top: mission,

not missionary. Can't jinx
purist locker room, killing field.

Show timidity, victory is history.
Yeah, machismo crops up —

tortured captives, bras panties booty,
fists trump words ... but free university.

*

Is tribal table talk a monologue?

Wife, fetch more tea chapatis.
Quick quick. *Yes, Sir.*

Only three eggs one milk jug left, wife? *Yes, Sir.*
Poached eggs white tea for my sons, me.

Yes, Sir. Naan dark tea for you, your girlies. *Yes, Sir.*

Why haven't you pressed our *shalwar kamiz,* washed

halls walls? *Yes, Sir.* Soaked beans,
cleaned latrine? Now, sweet cow. *Yes, Sir.*

Here's a contract for your extra dowry. *Yes, Sir.*
Put your X on this line; dare not decline. *Yes, Sir.*

Is that all you can say,
wife? *Yes, Sir.*

*

That's a soul-splat. Free-range chat
hotter than *burkas* dropped on demand.

Don't two worldly craniums
make a *hieros gamos*: sacred-union.

I hear in your voice, Malala, terror

renounced unfounded
enlivens Swat families grounded

in mutually toiled soil. Why can't
the perverse

see this worth.
Sever this serpentine-cycle.

It's contrived — like *Stepford Wives:*
husbands, craving certainty,

converted *The Wife* into robot, coiffed
kohl-eyed buffed.

*

Even laughter's *haram* in Swat.
Misery denies it recruits,

drains life-force. Your *Qari Sahib,*
Islamic teacher, preached

in strange Arabic. You pleaded for
a translation, loath to learn she

excused Benazir's death. Pupils
circling Bhutto's bus discovered

what agendas distort the Qur'an,
what verses resort to blessings

kindnesses, what marches
reinforce stoic activism.

*

I witnessed Indigenous Woman's Missing Sisters road show:

> Smudging, traipsing, shoeless, I hear
> all 1500 souls inside me crying out.
>
> In strange cars. On remote roads.
> In one-hour-rooms. On hypodermic highways.

In exquisitely beaded moccasins.
Two-sister-faces. Let there be Peace.

Angels: Missing Sisters. Sorrow.
Glitters in candlelight.

Existence fills industrial-strength jails.
These beaded cries. Catch light.

Refract far wide.
Run down our cheeks.

The wrong wails we are only guests in Sorrow's House:
our home *native* land.

*

Malala, in your language it's not
Wham, bam,

but *haram.*
Shazaam: when edicts inflict *burkas.*

When curves are impaled
by a lousy beard, stale skin from above.

When no love leaves man's lips, leavens his leer.
No *Open Sesame.*

Son-making is his blunt aim,
like this: thrust, grunt.

Friend to friend, genuine whole,
trumps tribalism, texting sexting.

*

Female friends tend me, feet firm
on the planet, smile sun-wide.

Longtime friend sunflower-high,
Linda had a *Near Death Experience.*

For her eulogy, I wrote
a poem for the loam we were giving her:

> Turquoise-copper perfection
> poured from your fingers.
>
> Kissing colours, your love birthed
> zany comments: twinkling wit.
>
> Whimsy enigmatic got-it grin.
> Full-voiced belly-laugh: you painted mirth.
>
> Georgian Bay   rock   wave   heron:
> immortalized after your last
>
> embattled breath. Sister, your letter
> between my visit, move here,
>
> a welcome mat. New province family,
> I only two years sober then.

In clothes given me I wear your spirit.
Forest my solace. Forest your *vision.*

*

Malala, you desired a tribute for your friends:
Shazia, Kainat — also shot on that bus.

Allahu Akbar for Skype — exiled,
it's your only contact with them.

Katerina Vaughan Fretwell, "Malala," 2016, watercolour, 15 x 11 inches.

Muhammad, Meccan

Malala, I've read the Qur'an and two
bios of your prophet Muhammad:

orphaned at six — Meccan parents dead,
unmoored without clan,

in ruins till harboured by Bedouins: the poor.
Tutoring him in caravan trade,

his older boss, widow Khadija, proposed
marriage. Never aloof,

over dictations on Gabriel's Mount Hira,
Khadija cradled The Prophet's

fear-driven quakes: *The Qur'an*
spoke to you — your terror is proof.

*

Though Moses, Jesus, Muhammad
vibrate higher than most people,

they couldn't resist the urge
to further The Word.

*

Meccans diluted their God's purity
with mediating deities, riffraff.

Muhammad's memoir devotional,
God breathed a hurricane, gusted inside him.

A ladder reeled to stars, like Jacob's.
Angels hosted his Ascension —

A Prophet in each heavenly rung.
Abraham welcomed him home.

                         *

I was uplifted fifty years ago
by a giant Ascension painting

in a provincial town.
The masterwork gave me vertigo.

Yet The Prophet threatened to cast down
Meccan capitalists on their own ground.

                         *

Tracked by Meccan assassins to Mount Thaur
he allowed adopted son Ali

to be his decoy, while he and an ally
deployed South to secure armed escort.

Bounty hunters alighting on Thaur but his Bedouin
power rescuing him with natural reverence:

spiders webbed the cave.
The hunters trudged on.

*

Leslie Hazelton's *The First Muslim*
fleshed out her own fascination,

devotion:

Aisha,
The Prophet's second wife,

dangled her toes in Muhammad's face,

teased out his grief

over his deceased first wife
Khadija.

She alone pleasured him

out of fatigue from pilgrims'

petitions.
Such tender rendering,
such faith.

*

Two decades after her Lord's death,
she led an army like *Joan of Arc*

mounted on red camel
in armoured howdah,

hurling war cries,
ignoring her pierced shoulder, aflame

with heavenly passion pain.
Her howdah prickled into

a porcupine of arrows. Don't forget
The Battle of the Camel,

where her volcanic chutzpah
fought for us — and fights for us
women, Malala.

*

I feel her with us. Defeated but undaunted,
writing up thousands of The Prophet's

actions prescriptions
on moral perturbation,

dictated to him on Mount Hira.
Women-hating clerics saving face by shaving

her testimony to hundreds. Precious lore lost,
like Alexandria's torched library,

the Bible's censored texts, unearthed
in a cave at Nag Hammadi.

What of Mary's missing missive?
Balanced worldviews curled up in smoke.

*

Barren, yes, but Aisha mantles Mother of the Faithful
to all newly manifested Muslims

imprints her fire on the final
Peoples of the Book —

instead of obedience, devotion dealt a gleeful twinkle.
We're dreamers. Be proud.

People of the Book

Malala,
this verse serves me well:

> *...if God had wished He could have made you*
> *one people.... So vie with one another in good works....*
>
> *He will then inform you of those things*
> *wherein ye differed.*

Why do believers smite each other?
Our three prophets vied over grains of sand:

Promised Land. Satan contained.
Dictation ingrained. What about the wind?

                    *

We are Word fleshed,
you and I. We love our Logos,

Abraham launching our lineage

of prophets tongue-harping

us into faith,
fealty like vintners

appraising grapes for luminosity.

Jesus portrays wine
a divine drink. We are ...

...Not for me. I'm done with grape
metaphors the Gospels semaphore.

For every vineyard good-deed,
there are lion-feeds, sword-crusades,

flaming stakes, witch-parades —
briar-patch of thorns, black capes,

rape by the thrall of alcohol.
No era, area escapes. A Talib shoots you,

yet you both have Pashtun roots. God.
Our inspired footage spools cruelty.

As if my beliefs float in the void.

Our metaphors can't teach. Screech
our fear Nothing's Out There, In Here.

Perverse? Mom ached to dump me
into the dumb-waiter after I asked

her friend to show me his stump.
I wasn't dumping; I was curious.

*

Allah winks
when you click
on your Bollywood flicks,
Malala.

*

I touch that numinous fire
in my woods walks

sharing intuitive thoughts
simplify rebuild

my derailed relationship
with earth — off-trail;

O Demeter,
mournful mother goddess,
your daughter Persephone,

I felt your rod, not
your love, I fled

to Hades' Merlot sea,
rebelling there by dispelling

privilege, bemoaning

goddess of home
hearth worship.

Remorse: we Book Peoples
sacrificed Abraham.

We so were drunk.

*

We're blinkered,
feverishly blind to divine

succour that would
shape us: our common

path is miracle,
Polaris our
guiding star.

*

We've come moon-riding far. I augured
as Aymara shaman;

you starred as Russian Tsar, Malala.
You placated Plato, I Scheherazade-d

for Nebuchadnezzar.
We own the night, sister. We've selected

every sect and cult —
Taoist monk,
Taliban recruit,

Anabaptist, Lakota Chief's
joy and grief.

*

I heard somewhere

Islam's Heaven
served up virgins
for Allah's martyrs.

Eden, enhanced,
danced where youth pampers

believers — slouching

on couches, plucking
figs,
apricots
olives, sucking

pure water, swathed in silk's
milk. Women also

repose in this enclosed tableau.
No I-phones, just Eye-Openers.

The Tao allots each Now and
Now and Now.

*

Disbelievers
will find out when, with iron collars

chains around their necks,
they are dragged

into scalding water, and then
burned in the fire.

Scribes delight in vivid
depictions of Eternal Night.

*

In the blazing flame, Malala,
scalding water slakes no thirst.

·Fruitless thorns ease no hunger,
endless flames spark no coolant.

Irrevocable fate flattens all
doubters, idolaters absorbed

in their own torments torrents.
If Allah is Love, we're loved.

I forgave myself my past drunkenness.
Seventy x Seventy pardons, Jesus said,

for my forested, pagan mind experiencing
soul in the sentience of all creatures.

*

As above, so below chant pagan worshippers.
Though still hated, we're at home

in many realms, finding soul
on earth sky. The whole

in one grain of sand. My Path is eclectic,
whole in the way one willow

warns its cohorts of tent-caterpillars
by extruding salicylic acid: *Sisters,*

sour your leaves to ward off pesters.
Once all women could talk to trees.

*

I still chant to forests, seeing *chi* —
silvery energy — pulsing around twig,

leaf, branch, bole. The whole.
I can't confine God to a box,

scrunch my beliefs into a dunce cap.
Jesus, Muhammad, Mary, Buddha

my avatars. Yet sinners
in our Scripted Hells

have no hope of parole: quaking, forsaken, they:
Scorch.   Scorn.

*

You me, miracles, Malala,
you overcame shots at close-range,

regaining your spirit-terrain.
I released booze, smokes, bile

to evoke my evolution,
growing inside, revising

a divine of my own devising —
not damned by god Out There,

Sky High but restored
by god/dess In Here and By.

With life's second chance,
let's dervish, let's dance.

*

We are already dancing.

Look, God and Prophet.

*

To Lilith, Mary.

To Hestia, Demeter.

In our dervish, let's invite
Allah, Goddess, feisty Aisha.

We form a circle.
Always moving.

Round as Ouroboros, ancient snake nipping its tail,
let's dance to Women in God and Prophet like this.

Nobility

You said *This award is for my powerful sisters*
whose voices need to be heard

in your Nobel Peace Prize
Acceptance Speech, Malala…

*

Lifting off from infancy onward,
your capacious brain sifted out

the bitter bullets of a maimed man,
nourishing rippling rings,

once silenced, hapless girls
in the hinterland Third World.

*

I too rejoice, at grouted-bricks
slicked into actual classrooms,

at blackboards beckoning
hordes of Mogadishu pupils,

chalky fingers flying over slate.
I too rejoice at AIDS widows' new fate —

re-purposed as Johar teachers.
We sing our gratitude to them.

*

Youngest winner. First girl. First Pashtun.
Sometimes our world spins it right.

Every girl schooled is a Singularity
eclipsing our rending disparity.

Globe's blood-red-trend
completely obsolete.

*

You added ... *the Nobel Committee believe(s)*
education is the best weapon

through which we can fight poverty,
ignorance and terrorism. Yes.

*

Micro-miracles for Kenyan mothers
unearthing the silenced and shamed,

unable to read manuals for survival:
contracts   labels   roadsigns   slogans   prices   cautions.

As if written in blood, braille — *ferengi*
in their own village, vale, *ferengi!*

*

Distended stomachs, mauled genitalia, lesion-ed skin:
your beam tunnels through

CARE-carton houses, malarial
water, sewage runnels. Literate Malala.

*

Your goal: moulding the global, tilling
to grow four billion dollars

to place *all girls* behind desks,
becoming mothers of the world,

rototiller teamed with Ugandan students
while summits stagnate under magnates

plumped on ornate rose-beds.
Your lost home, fathomless ghost.

*

Shot, reviled, exiled,
You are the word we are.

Katerina Vaughan Fretwell, *"Self-Portrait Ochre Epiphanies,"* 2016,
acrylic 20 x 16 inches.

We Are Malala

Daughters of the world, you were shot in Swat
yet woke in Birmingham.

Bullets blitzed your brains,
splintered bone,

strafing your cerebellums into swelling.
Pieces of skull, excised and inserted

under your stomachs till safe to reinsert.
Coma courted to avert compression

sudden consciousness could cause.
You're only fifteen, daughters;

you're all Malala now. Dearest walkers
in the footsteps of the first hand writing,

Head Mullah proclaims you were shot,
not for demanding schooling, but

praising Obama for rising
to realize his dreams.

*

Malala, you forgave your shooter. Do you, daughters?
Dr Fiona, skilled in moving gravely ill children, feared

if you die, she'd be blamed for killing
Pakistan's Mother Teresa. So you awoke,

groggy, to English-speaking doctors,
white foggy world, red brick

row houses, no anchoring loam,
no taste smell of home.

Dr Fiona gave you a white teddy bear
you saw as malachite-green. Who pays for all this

shine probe screen,
you wondered.

Forgave your shooter,
yet pined for family,

quaked, who could you trust?

O my *jani*, O my *pisho!*
Told not to sob. How could you not. You'd been robbed.

*

At ten percent healed, your face half-concealed:
your speech regressed, your right eye recessed,

your scalp bald, your mouth listed left,
you forgave your shooter.

*

Ziauddin, your dad, claimed rogues stole your grin.
You forgave your shooter Ataulah Khan,

yet your dear bus driver and
school accountant paid a penalty.

Lopsided justice.
Yet you forgive even this.

*

The UN named November 10, *Malala Day* —
one month, one day, after the shooting.

However, you rooted for next day's
operation to repair

your facial nerve. Eight and a half hours,
many bone fragments scoured,

removed, three more
drab months of

rehab for you to think make
a smile, a wink, *yet*

you forgave your shooter
in your stubbornness.

*

December 6, at the Botanical Gardens,
you sang a canticle to the shock of home:

before your eyes, Swat Valley flora.
Pakistan footed your $600,000

medical
bills, scooted over to Ziauddin,

diplomatic passport   (he can't seek
asylum)

and an education job.

At The Mall,
you were appalled at male-female

chats, hand-holding, kissing,
bare-legged

ex-pats. Skull piece
too thin to reinsert, you wear

a titanium plate and cochlear implant —
bionic; miracles.

                                        *

Ataulah aimed at a spot   point-blank.
A miracle is what he got. It talks.

                                        *

Rental house so forlorn, piano so foreign.
Huge rooms an echo corridor —

no villagers warming the walls,
strange tongue, customs.

Your own *Allahu Akbar*
moment, His to impart: resilient brain, hug-worthy heart,

two eyes for bright-sights, two lips for love-quips
two feet for greetings, two ears

for endearments, a nose for homegrown roses.
You plead: *Forgive my shooter.*

*

How blithe. At Sunapee, New Hampshire,
Nineteen Sixty-One, five cousins

heading to a cottage bash were stopped dead
by Mom: *You can all stay in at least one night.*

So we did, intuitively attuned to her grave tone.
Mom didn't single us out by name.

She expressed what it took to be a role-model
citizen: community-builder.

*

Mom reminds me of Ziauddin.
He instilled your thrill at fixing the jinxed.

*

Later I witnessed Mom roll her eyes heavenward;
this her fourth final spiral — cancer

lodged in her lungs onward;
age 53, in late August. On May 18,

Nineteen Sixty-Two, during my finals,
at age 17, while I applied myself

for my graduation, Mom died. 54.

Now 70 plus, I've charted through the arts,
mentoring 12-step women,

honouring Mom's *Farewell Speech*.
What you, Malala, do.

*

United we thrive, divided we die.
All souls. All sentience.

*

Sentenced to prescience, *We Are Malala*.

Notes

"Star Blessed and Crossed":

1. Quote from the Qur'an taken from *The Qur'an: A New Translation* by M.A.S. Abdel Haleem, 2004. All quotes from the Qur'an are taken from this text.
2. General Zia ul-Haq seized power in a military coup in 1977 and enforced Sharia strictness
3. "The Road Not Taken" by Robert Frost, *Mountain Interval* (1916).
4. Qur'an 22:39.
5. "The Real Danger for Women on Campus," by Anne Kingston, *Macleans*, December 2, 2013.
6. *The Prophet* by Kahlil Gibran. "To experience joy, one must know sorrow."

"To Allah, in a Bottle"

1. John Stuart Mill, *On Liberty,* 1859 (chapter 1).
2. Mary Wollstonecraft, *A Vindication of the Rights of Woman,* 1790, (chapter 5).
3. Savonarola was a book-burning medieval monk.
4. Sally Armstrong, *Veiled Threat: The Hidden Power of the Women of Afghanistan* (2002).
5. Qur'an 4:34.
6. "Pakistan deadliest country for a journalist," by Manzoor Ali, *New Internationalist*, May 2012.
7. Kurt Eichenwald, *500 Days, Lies and Secrets in the Terror Wars,* (2012).

"Short Shrift and Swat Shot Sestina"

1. *pur laine,* Quebecois expression for ethnic purity.
2. *Sacre Bleu, Hosti de Tabernac,* Quebecois swear words directed against the church and the Eucharistic communion wafer.
3. Trayvon Martin, unarmed African-American killed by a cop in a gated community. Cop acquitted.
4. Family photograph featured in *I Am Malala.* Photographer and copyright, Antonio Olmos.

"Arma(geddon) Get Going"

1. MindCraft, video game to create buildings, trees, animals, etc., all in rectangular shapes.
2. "Wardrobe malfunction," journalist's phrase for Janet Jackson's bared breast at football halftime.
3. Muhammad's apocalyptic signs, discussed in Leslie Hazelton's *The First Muslim* (2013).
4. "Jarring," *The Bell Jar,* autobiography of confessional poet Sylvia Plath (1963).
5. U.S. president Donald Trump surrounded himself with avowed white supremacists.
6. *Canadian Living* is a magazine.
7. *Schadenfreude* means delight in someone's misfortune.

"How It Starts"

1. "Sound and Fury," *Macbeth,* Shakespeare, Act 5, Scene 5
2. William Faulkner, *The Sound and the Fury* (1929).
3. Qur'an 4:24.

"Wham, Bam, *Haram*"

1. *Allahu Ackbar,* God is Greater. Irshad Manji, *The Trouble with Islam* (2003).
2. "Military … punishes," Noemi Mercier and Alec Castonguay, "Our Military Disgrace," *Macleans* 127 (2014): 20.
3. "Sixteen years ago…," Jane O'Hara, "A war with no end in sight," ibid.
4. *Stepford Wives,* 1970's movie about husbands turning wives into robots.

"Muhammad, Meccan"

1. Information on Khadija, Mount Thaur and Aisha from Leslie Hazelton's *The First Muslim* (2013).

"People of the Book"

1. Qur'an 5:48.
2. Qur'an 40:70–72

"Nobility"

1. Malala Yousafzai's Nobel Acceptance Speech, October 10, 2014.
2. *Ferengi* means stranger.

"We Are Malala"

1. *Jani* means dear one; *pisho* means cat—both are terms of endearment, from *I Am Malala* (2013) (Glossary, 316, 317).

Artwork credits:

Painting on page xii is inspired by the photo by Insiya Syed from *We Are Displaced: My Journey and Stories from Refugee Girls around the World* by Malala Yousafzai with Liz Welch (2019).

Painting on page 27 is inspired by the family photo by Antonio Olmos from *I Am Malala: The Story of the Girl Who Stood Up for Education and was Shot by the Taliban,* by Malala Yousafzai, with Christina Lamb (2013).

Acknowledgements

Dedicated to Malala and to everyone, particularly girls, struggling to get an education, to my family who believed in the importance of an education and to my legions of teachers/mentors.

Huge gratitude above all to my editor *non pareil*, Harold Rhenisch, who pulled me out of the politics and into the poetry and to the following friends and cohorts who read or heard various drafts: Penn Kemp, Susan McCaslin, Doyali Farah Islam, Sandra Harris, Dianna and Douglas Allen, Dave Bartlett, Shelly Hazzard, Charlotte Hurd, Brenda Muller, Pat Poole. Also huge kudos to Luciana Ricciutelli and Renée Knapp of Inanna, my incomparable publisher and publicist respectively.

Credits (poems previously published, listed under their original titles before being compressed into ten long poems for this book):

"Missing Sisters" – *Feminist Caucus Anthology,* League of Canadian Poets, 2014; *Subterranean Blue,* 2014; *Mindshadows Anthology*, 2014
"Malala and Me" – *Scarlet Thistle Anthology,* 2014
"To Linda France Bulger" – *Eulogy,* 2014
"Wheeling Dealing" – *Prairie Journal,* 2015
"New Deal" – *Prairie Journal,* 2015
"Portents" – *Prairie Journal,* 2015
"Sacrificial Gods" – *Prairie Journal,* 2015
"To Aisha" – *Prairie Journal,* 2015
"We Are Malala," part 4 – *Prairie Journal,* 2015, nominated for a Pushcart Prize
"Short Shrift and Swat Shot Sestina" – *The Windsor Review,* 2017.

Photo: Alan Clark

Katerina Vaughan Fretwell's recent poetry collections, *Angelic Scintillations* (2011), *Class Acts* (2013), and *Dancing on a Pin* (2015), published by Inanna, include her art work. Her award-winning poetry has appeared in journals and anthologies in Canada, Denmark, Japan, United States, and Wales. Her sestina, "Kissing Cousins," was shortlisted for *Descant Magazine's* Winston Collins Poetry Prize, 2012. Five poems from *Dancing on a Pin* were finalists in *subTerrain's* Lush Triumphant Poetry Contest, 2015. *Dancing on a Pin* was also shortlisted for the 2016 Pat Lowther Memorial Award for poetry. Recent poems are included in *Heartwood,* edited by Lesley Strutt, and *Another Dysfunctional Cancer Poem Anthology*, edited by Priscila Uppal and Meaghan Strimas. Fretwell chaired the 2005 Lowther Jury Prize and edited two anthologies for the Feminist Caucus, League of Canadian Poets, 2004 and 2006. She lives in Seguin, Ontario.